THE
HEALING
POWER
OF NUTS

Writer
Michele Price Mann
Consultant
Diane L. McKay, Ph.D., F.A.C.N.

Publications International, Ltd.

Cover Photo: Photodisc

Writer:
Michele Price Mann is a freelance writer from Birmingham, Alabama. Mann has been writing about health and nutrition topics for more than a decade, and she enjoys helping readers make sense of the latest research.

Consultant:
Diane L. McKay, Ph.D., F.A.C.N., is a scientist in the Antioxidants Research Laboratory at the Jean Mayer USDA Human Nutrition Research Center on Aging at Tufts University and an adjunct assistant professor at Tufts University's Friedman School of Nutrition Science and Policy in Boston. She is a member of the American Society for Nutrition and a fellow of the American College of Nutrition.

Table of Contents

Go Nuts for Better Health

Take a look at many of the products you use every day and you'll see a trend: Concentrated is in. Whether it's laundry soap, drink mixes, or cell phones, we're getting more in smaller packages. But nature perfected this formula long ago—just look at nuts. These tiny fruits are tasty, portable treats, but they're also loaded with tons of healthful elements.

An alarm probably just went off in your head because you've heard nuts are also loaded with fat, and as a result, calories. However, you'll soon discover that the fat found in nuts has all kinds of benefits for your body, including fighting off heart disease, stroke, and possibly certain types of cancer.

This book explores the effects of nuts on several serious health conditions. Keep in mind, though, that the information here is intended to complement, not replace, proper medical care and the advice of a health-care professional. Be sure to discuss with your physician the benefits of including nuts in your diet.

Nuts: A Natural Wonder

Whether you enjoy nuts straight out of their shells, as part of your favorite recipes, or smeared on bread as nut butter, these tasty treats work much harder for you than you might realize. It's time to crack the case and find out what makes nuts so great.

Nuts are packed with muscle-building protein and essential vitamins and minerals. Maybe you've been avoiding these tasty treats because you've heard they are high in fat. That's true, but the fats they harbor are the good-for-you mono- and polyunsaturated kinds. They also contain essential, heart-helping omega-3 fatty acids. Plus, because they are plant foods, nuts do not contain the cholesterol found in animal sources of protein.

We'll explore all those facts a bit later, but first we need to answer a few simple questions. Although you may think you know exactly what nuts are, you'll probably be surprised by how many different categories they actually fit into.

The Hard Truth About Nuts

Nuts have a bit of an identity crisis. Botanically, a nut is a fruit, but botanists will tell you that some of what are labeled "nuts" on your grocer's shelf are misidentified. They aren't *true* nuts in the scientific sense. Many of the nuts in your local market are considered seeds or kernels, and some nuts don't fall into either category. For example, peanuts are considered legumes, like peas.

However, if you ask chefs or registered dietitians, they would tell you not to be so picky. To them, taste, texture, and nutritional content matter much more than the intricacies of scientific classification.

A Nut by Any Other Name

Some of the confusion about nuts can be blamed on the English, who in about the 7th century A.D. started using the word "nut" to describe any hard kernel. Most etymologists (language historians) believe the word comes from the Indo-European word *knuk*, which means "lump."

Botanical Nuts & Bolts

Because true nuts are scientifically categorized as tree fruits, that puts walnuts in the same category as apples. The two fruits differ in the way their outer casing, or ovary, ripens. With a nut, the ovary hardens as it ripens and becomes a shell. Inside the shell, the fruit's seed, or kernel, develops. With certain types of nuts, that seed becomes an edible treasure. (With other fruits, the ovary develops into a more delicate skin that protects the soft flesh.) Although nuts contain seeds, most seeds are not, from a botanical standpoint, true nuts. Most of the "nuts" you eat (except for peanuts) are actually the seeds of tree nuts.

There are many classifications of tree nuts, but most of them don't have delicacies hidden within their shells. Of the 11 types of nut trees—wingnut, beech, oak, stone oak, alder, birch, hornbeam, walnut, pecan, chestnut, and hazelnut (filbert)—only the last four produce edible seeds. The beauty of a tree nut is that the shell acts as a natural preservative and protects the seed from disease and from the elements.

Dining Definition

From a purely culinary standpoint (as well as from the perspective of this book), the definition of a nut is painted in much broader strokes. Food experts classify nuts as any edible kernels encased in shells.

From Plant to Plate

When adding walnuts to your favorite bread recipe or popping peanuts at the ball game, you probably don't give a second thought to the nut's journey from the earth to your mouth. But the process of growing and gathering nuts is fascinating and is unique to each plant. We'll take a look at how it happens for a few popular varieties.

Acquiring almonds. The blooming of beautiful white flowers on almond trees, which in the northern hemisphere usually happens in February and March, marks the beginning of the process that will eventually produce delectable almonds. Although the flowers are enticing, you don't want to get too close: Once the flowers bloom, growers depend on bees to do the pollination

Will the Real Nut Please Stand Up?

From a scientific standpoint, most popular nuts can't claim to be true nuts. See if your favorites are really nutty and which have a secret identity.

- **True nuts:** Walnut, Pecan, Hazelnut, Chestnut

- **Seeds:** Almond, Brazil Nut, Cashew, Pine Nut, Pistachio

- **Kernel:** Macadamia Nut

- **Legume:** Peanut

work because the trees can't pollinate themselves like other fruit plants.

If pollinated successfully, a grayish-green fruit will begin to appear as the flowers fade. This fruit, also known as a drupe, will begin the growing and drying process during the late summer months. Almonds are ready for harvesting in early fall. Once the fruit has matured and the hull, or dried outer casing of the fruit, begins to open, the almond is ready to be processed. Mechanical tree shakers coax the nuts from their home, and they are gathered and separated for the harvesters' specific needs.

Almonds grow best in climates that have hot summers and warm winters. They require a bit of frost to encourage flowers to bloom, but temperate climates are best. Italy, Spain, the Middle East, parts of Australia, and South Africa all have great climates for almond cultivation, but California's Central Valley, a 450-mile stretch of land that covers much of the central area of the Golden State, has an ideal climate for

Did You Know...

Almonds are more closely related to peaches and plums than to other tree nuts, such as walnuts.

almond growing. In fact, according to the California Almond Board, the state is the world's leading almond producer and is responsible for 80 percent of the entire planet's almonds.

What about walnuts? Two types of walnuts are grown and eaten around the world: the English walnut (which is also known as the Persian walnut) and the black walnut. Most of the walnuts you find at your local grocery store are the English ones, which have a thinner shell and a larger nut. Black walnuts have tough shells and don't taste as good as English walnuts.

Black walnuts grow throughout the eastern United States, but English walnuts favor a more mild environment. Early settlers in America tried to grow English walnuts in Pennsylvania and Massachusetts, but the walnuts floundered. However, when the nuts were planted

Beware of Falling Nuts

If you plan to start collecting Brazil nuts, you might want to invest in a hard hat. Brazil nuts grow on gigantic trees (up to 150 feet tall) in the Amazon basin. Nut collectors must wait for calm days to gather nuts, or they risk being pummeled by the four- to six-inch pods.

in the more temperate areas of California, they flourished. According to the Food and Agriculture Organization of the United Nations, the United States produces 20 percent of the world's walnuts (primarily English walnuts). China grows the most, followed by the United States, Iran, Turkey, Ukraine, and Romania.

Walnuts are harvested in the fall. When the nuts are ripe, the outer hull, or husk, splits open and the walnut falls to the ground. To get the more reluctant walnuts, growers use mechanical shakers to wiggle the nuts loose. The walnuts are then allowed to dry before they are shelled and processed.

Producing pecans. Many of the states south of the Mason–Dixon Line are perfect for the pecan. The South's mild winters and hot, humid summers provide ideal conditions for the tastiest of these tree nuts. As a result, the United States produces 80 percent of the world's pecans, according to the National Pecan Shellers Association. The United States Department of Agriculture (USDA) reports that 76 percent of those are grown in the South.

In a natural environment, pecans fall from their protective hulls once they ripen, but when the nuts are cultivated, mechanical shakers do that job. This happens sometime between April and July, depending on where the trees are grown.

The one and only peanut. The peanut is a unique member of the nut family. To start with, peanuts aren't tree fruits, seeds, or kernels. Peanuts are legumes that trace their roots to the pea family (thus the descriptive name) and grow underground on a vine instead of on a tree.

Peanuts grow best in warm climates with mild winters, which makes the American South an ideal location. According to the

> **Did You Know...**
>
> The plant that produces cashews is closely related to poison ivy.

American Peanut Council, seven Southern states (ranked in order of production, greatest to least: Georgia, Texas, Alabama, North Carolina, Florida, Virginia, and Oklahoma) account for 99 percent of all American-grown peanuts. The United States is the third-largest producer of peanuts in the world, right behind China and India.

Peanuts are usually planted in the late spring, and after most of the pods have matured, a mechanical "digger" loosens the soil around the pods, and a "shaker" sifts away the soil. The pods are allowed to dry in the sun for a few days and then a peanut combine separates the vines from the pods. The pods are cured to remove moisture in order to increase storage time, and then the cured pods are inspected, cleaned, and sorted according to size. About half of the peanuts produced in the United States get used for peanut butter. The others are used for snack foods or as candy ingredients.

No matter how you enjoy your peanuts or any other nut, you can do so without guilt, as long as you eat them in moderation. In coming chapters, you'll find out why dietitians and doctors alike are saying it's okay to be crazy about nuts.

When Nuts Make You Sick

About 3 million people in the United States are affected by nut allergies, according to the American Academy of Allergy, Asthma, and Immunology. Nut allergies can cause hives, a runny nose, itchy eyes and throat, or even nausea and vomiting. In more serious cases, a severe allergic reaction called anaphylaxis is triggered. Anaphylaxis can be life-threatening and can cause swelling of the tongue and throat, constriction of the airway to the lungs, and a drop in blood pressure. If you eat nuts and begin to notice any adverse reaction, get medical help immediately.

Nuts Have Never Been Better

From prehistoric man to ancient royalty to medieval peasants to supermarket shoppers of today, nuts have been a reliable food source throughout history. Unfortunately, because nuts contain so much fat, they have fallen out of favor with the American public in the past few decades. However, newer research is restoring faith in nuts.

A recent archeological excavation in Israel found remnants of seven types of nuts and a variety of primitive nutcrackers that scientists believe date back 780,000 years. A dig in Iraq uncovered evidence of nut consumption that dates back to 50,000 B.C. And in Texas, pecan shells were unearthed near human artifacts that may date back to 6000 B.C.

It's easy to see why nuts have been so popular through the ages. You don't have to track and kill a nut. In fact, nuts were one of the first convenience foods; not only could they be carried, but their ability to be stored for months at a time made them great for long, harsh winters. Nuts are also rich in fat and protein, which make them filling and nourishing. And their versatility means you can eat them right out of the shell, press them for oil, or mash them to make nut butter.

Ancient Nuts

One of the first recorded references to nuts is in the Bible. On their second journey to Egypt, Joseph's brothers brought almonds and pistachios to trade for grain. And in Numbers 17, Aaron's rod miraculously buds and bears almonds, proving he is God's chosen priest.

Almonds were a dietary mainstay of the ancient people of the Middle East; they ate sweet almonds (there are two types of almond plants, sweet and bitter; bitter almonds are used for oil and extracts) blanched, roasted, sliced, or ground. The Romans were the first to make candied almonds, and they often gave these treats as wedding presents as a symbol

Did You Know...

Romans believed eating bitter almonds while drinking would make wine's effects less potent. Although almonds are a tasty complement to wine, they won't keep you sober.

of fertility (a tradition still carried on today). In the Middle Ages, almonds were ground into flour, and many recipes called for almond "milk," a drink made from ground almonds, water, and typically some sort of sweetener. Almond oil was used as medicine in many European and Middle Eastern cultures before the time of Christ. Fans of natural medicine still use it today for treating indigestion, as a laxative, and for easing coughs and laryngitis.

Pistachios also have an intriguing history. In the Bible, Jacob's sons favored pistachios, and some say they were one of the Queen of Sheba's favorite foods. According to one pistachio legend, lovers who meet under a pistachio tree on a moonlit night will find good luck if they hear the nuts crack.

Pistachios probably originated in an area that stretches from West Asia through Turkey. Romans introduced pistachios to Europe from Asia sometime around the 1st century A.D. The nuts didn't arrive in the United States until the late 19th century, and it wasn't until the 1930s that pistachios became a popular American snack food.

The history of walnuts (in this case the English walnut) is as old as the stories of almonds and pistachios. In fact, ancient inscriptions suggest walnut trees were grown in the Hanging Gardens of Babylon. Walnuts were also a valued staple in the diet of ancient Greeks and Romans.

The walnut even has a place in Greek mythology, as the god Dionysus turned his love, Carya, into a walnut tree after she died. Romans also considered walnuts food for the gods, while mere mortal citizens of Rome used walnut oil and walnut flour. Walnut oil was used extensively in the Middle Ages, and peasants

A Colorful History

If you come across a pistachio straight from the tree, you'll have a khaki-colored shell with a green nut inside. In the early 20th century, a Brooklyn street vendor, trying to find a niche in the growing pistachio market, decided to dye his pistachios red. The red color caught the eyes of bystanders and made the nuts more appealing by covering any imperfections. The red pistachios were so popular other vendors started using the crimson color on their pistachios. Today, only about 15 percent of pistachios available on the market are still dyed red, mainly because the red fad ran its course and newer harvesting techniques now result in fewer blemishes and stains.

ground up walnut shells to make bread. Walnuts made their way to the New World sooner than pistachios, arriving with Spanish priests in California during the 18th century.

The tough-shelled black walnut hit the world stage much later than its thin-shelled relative. This variety is also known as the American walnut and is believed to be native to North America. Historical records indicate black walnut wood was shipped to England from Virginia in about 1610. During the mid-19th century, black walnut wood became quite fashionable, but the tree was already becoming rare. The wood experienced a revival in popularity in the 1970s, but on account of changing tastes and higher cost, the demand for black walnut wood

The Many Names of the Walnut

Walnuts come in two main varieties, the English walnut and the black walnut. The English walnut is also known as the Persian walnut. The Persian walnut got its moniker simply because it grows well in the Middle East. The English title has a more interesting background. When ship trade became more extensive, English sailors would use walnuts to barter when they traveled around the Mediterranean.

dropped. As far as the nut itself goes, the black walnut is sweet, but not as popular as the English variety. Today the black walnut is used more widely in flavorings, such as black walnut ice cream.

Chestnuts, first mentioned by the ancient Greeks and Romans, were a major part of Middle Eastern and European diets for centuries. People also used chestnuts as medicine because they were believed to fend off rabies and dysentery. But their primary role was as a durable food source for people who lived in areas where winters were harsh and food was scarce. Chestnuts are a bit difficult to find today, except around Thanksgiving, but they are a treat for those who discover them.

Newer Nuts

Although scientists discovered pecan remnants in Texas that date back to 6000 B.C., written historical references to the pecan go back only to about the 16th century. The first settlers on America's shores most likely learned about pecans from Native Americans. Spanish colonists in northern Mexico were cultivating pecans in the early 18th century, and the first pecan tree planting in what would become the United States took place on Long Island, New York, in 1772. As America devel-

The Peanut King

Peanut-lovers owe a debt of gratitude to George Washington Carver. Carver was a botanist and agricultural scientist who taught and conducted research at Tuskegee University from 1896 until his death in 1943. During that time, he discovered more than 300 uses for the peanut, ranging from the edible, including peanut milk, to the more out-of-the-ordinary, such as dyes, shoe polish, and shaving cream. But Carver's main contribution to the peanut, and to agriculture, was his encouragement of Southern farmers to rotate their crops. Growing cotton is hard on the soil, but alternating between growing peanuts and cotton helps the land recover. This rotating crop cycle revolutionized farming in the South.

oped into a nation, pecan cultivation spread south to the Gulf of Mexico region, and the nut became an important commodity. In fact, founding fathers George Washington and Thomas Jefferson grew pecan trees. Pecans were so valuable in the early 19th century that they were more profitable to grow than cotton in some areas.

As with pecans, evidence exists that peanuts have been around for millennia, but the first recorded mentions of the peanut date back only to the 16th century, when explorers began poking around the New World. Peanuts probably originated in South America, but the nuts came to North America via Africa. Spanish explorers took peanuts from South America back to Spain, and from Spain the nuts went to Asia and Africa. Peanuts became a common crop in Africa, so when Africans were brought as slaves to North America, they brought the peanut with them.

People originally grew peanuts as food for pigs, but they started eating peanuts themselves by the late 19th century. In addition, peanuts were used for oil and even as a cocoa substitute. But because they were difficult to grow and were stereotyped as poor peoples' food, peanuts weren't widely grown for human consumption until the early 20th century. Better equipment made growing and harvesting the crops easier, and different uses of the peanut, including peanut butter and peanut candy, helped increase its popularity.

Is It Okay to Go Nuts?

Low-fat diets were all the rage in the 1990s. Books that touted the benefits of lowering your overall fat intake filled bookstores. Shoppers saw new low-fat

From Spa to Sandwich

Many people, including George Washington Carver, are credited with inventing peanut butter. However, the spread that crudely resembles what you have in your pantry most likely debuted in the late 19th century. In 1890, a man named George A. Bayle, Jr., sold peanut butter as a protein substitute for people who had bad (or no) teeth. In 1895, John Harvey Kellogg obtained the first patent for making peanut butter. Peanut butter became a delicacy for the wealthy at the turn of the 20th century, and it was sold as a health food in spas and fancy tearooms. As peanut production became easier and peanuts more abundant, peanut butter entered mainstream America. Once sugar was added to peanut butter to improve flavor and commercially available sliced bread was invented in 1928, the popularity of peanut butter soared.

versions of their favorite products, including cookies and potato chips, on just about every shelf in the supermarket.

But the low-fat craze left nuts on the food fringe. Because nuts are naturally high in fat, it's virtually impossible to create low-fat versions. Besides, who would want to eat a handful of nuts when, for the same number of calories and half the fat, you could eat eight low-fat chocolate cookies? The government even turned a deaf ear to the health benefits of nuts. The first five editions of *Dietary Guidelines for Americans* (published in 1980, 1985, 1990, 1995, and 2000), issued jointly by the United States Department of Agriculture (USDA) and the United States Department of Health and Human Services (HHS), barely mentioned nuts in an overview of healthful foods.

Experts began taking a new look at fat around the turn of the 21st century. Nutritionists and researchers had long focused on the negatives of fat, but they'd neglected the benefits. New studies prove that it's the *types* of fat you eat that matters. The right kinds, eaten in moderation, can actually make you healthier. As public policy began catching up with the latest scientific findings, the government changed its recommendations—finally recognizing nuts as an integral part of a healthful diet.

Shaping the Way America Eats

The USDA and HHS started publishing *Dietary Guidelines for Americans* to help health professionals and health educators combat obesity and other health issues related to Americans' generally poor

eating habits. The USDA and HHS base their recommendations on the newest scientific research,
so to keep up with changing data, the government
decided to update *Dietary Guidelines for Ameri-*
cans every five years. In the first five editions, the
guidelines focused mostly on total fat intake, but
they did separate saturated fat (the bad kind) from
unsaturated fat (the
good kind) and encour-
aged eating foods that
are low in cholesterol.

In 1992, the USDA
released the first Food
Guide Pyramid to offer
Americans practical ways to apply the guidelines.
The Food Guide Pyramid prompted many Americans to take a closer look at the amount of fat in
their diets. It also sparked a new market for low-fat
foods, and consumers had an array of choices they
never had before. However, Americans were con-
tinuing to gain weight because although they were
getting fewer calories from fat, they were loading
up on carbohydrate calories, and not reducing
total calories overall. The rates of chronic health
problems related to being overweight, such as
heart disease and type 2 diabetes, increased, too.

Did You Know...

The peanut
butter and
jelly sandwich
was officially
invented in 1901.

Crunching Nut Numbers

Here's the breakdown on the calorie and fat content of popular nuts, based on a one-and-a-half-ounce (⅓ cup) serving.

Nut	Calories	Total Grams of Fat
Almond	246	21.5
Brazil nut	279	28.3
Cashew	235	18.7
Chestnut	104	0.9
Hazelnut	267	25.8
Macadamia	305	32.2
Peanut	241	20.9
Pecan	294	30.6
Pine nut	286	29.0
Pistachio	237	18.9
Walnut	278	27.7

Source: U.S. Department of Agriculture, Agricultural Research Service. USDA Nutrient Data Laboratory. USDA National Nutrient Database for Standard Reference; 2006: Release 19.

The focus on lowering overall fat consumption alone wasn't working.

The USDA and HHS overhauled the Food Guide Pyramid in 2005 when they released the sixth edition of *Dietary Guidelines for Americans*. The new pyramid, "MyPyramid," put more emphasis on the benefits of healthful fats. These new fat recommendations still encourage eating foods low in saturated fat and cholesterol, and they include a recommendation to lower intake of *trans* fatty acids, the worst kind of fat for you (the next chapter has more information about *trans* fat). The 2005 editions of MyPyramid and *Dietary Guidelines for Americans* also reflected new research about the benefits of unsaturated fats and essential fatty acids—great news for nut-lovers.

What You Need

Because nuts are plant sources of fat, they are full of good-for-you monounsaturated and polyunsaturated fat, are cholesterol-free (unlike animal sources of fat), and are a good source of protein. Unsaturated fats are beneficial because they help keep your arteries healthy and help lower cholesterol levels. Some nuts (particularly walnuts) are also a good source of another type of heart-healthful unsaturated fat: omega-3 fatty acids. Studies are showing that omega-3 fatty acids can help lower cholesterol and blood-pressure levels, as well as reduce the risk of heart attack and stroke (see the next chapter for more details).

Nuts are also surprisingly good sources of vitamin E, which is considered an antioxidant nutrient. Antioxidants inhibit oxidation, a natural body process that causes cell damage, and have been linked to a lowered risk for several chronic diseases, including heart disease and some cancers. Nuts are also rich in potassium and magnesium, minerals that help the body function at its best by regulating blood pressure and keeping muscles and nerves working properly. Nuts are

How Fat Works for You

Fat is essential because it helps the body absorb and use certain vitamins (vitamins A, D, E, and K are fat-soluble vitamins). Fat helps children grow and keeps skin healthy. Fat gives your organs an internal cushion and acts as the body's insulation. And the energy from fat lasts longer than the energy from other nutrients. This is because it takes longer for your body to metabolize, and because it has more calories per gram (nine) than either protein or carbohydrates (four each).

high in fiber, which can help lower cholesterol levels. While fats from meat and other animal sources are discouraged, the newest version of *Dietary Guidelines for Americans* specifically recommends including nuts and nut butters (even as an occasional replacement for meat) as part of an overall healthful diet.

Research continues to find amazing benefits to eating nuts. Nuts are good for your heart—so good that the U.S. Food and Drug Administration approved a health claim for nuts that states including "a moderate amount of nuts in an overall healthy diet may reduce the risk of heart disease." Nuts are also full of naturally occurring phytochemicals (substances produced by plants that help defend people against disease) that have been associated with protection against cancer, diabetes, and other chronic health problems.

Did You Know...

Cashews have a toxic oil between the shell and the nut. Before nuts can be sold, they must be shelled and roasted to remove any remnant of the poisonous oil.

Making Nuts Count

A few nuts go a long way. *Dietary Guidelines for Americans* recommends eating one-and-a-half ounces (about one-third cup) of nuts four to five times a week. Depending on the nut, that can mean 104 to 305 calories and 1 gram to more than 32 grams of fat per serving (see "Crunching Nut Numbers" on page 25 for more information).

But don't panic, fat phobics. Although that seems like a lot of fat, remember that nuts are full of the types of fat that are actually beneficial to the body. Plus, nuts contain essential nutrients that are vital for good health. One look at the healing effects of nuts in the following chapter and you'll be adding nuts back to your menu.

G'day, Macadamia

Most people associate the macadamia nut with Hawaii, but the nut is originally from Australia. Some enterprising Americans tasted the nut on a visit down under, and somewhere around the late 19th century, introduced the nut to Hawaii.

Great Things Come in Small Packages

Recent research has absolved nuts of their junk-food status. Studies show that eating a handful of nuts on most days of the week can do wonders for your heart and might lower your risk of developing diabetes, protect you against certain cancers, and provide other health benefits.

If you've shelved your favorite shelled treats because they didn't fit in your low-fat diet, think again, because there is much more to nuts than fat. The fact is nuts are chock-full of good-for-you unsaturated fat, protein, fiber, and essential vitamins and minerals. The key to making nuts a valuable part of your healthful eating plan is understanding what makes them so good for you, starting with their most-feared element: fat.

Fat 101

Fat is at the center of most diet debates because it packs a big calorie punch. One gram of fat holds nine calories, while one gram of carbohydrate or protein carries four calories. Thus, the more fat you eat, the more calories you consume. We know nuts are high in fat, yet they are considered very nutritious. So does that mean eating a high-fat diet is better? Yes and no—it depends on the type of fat you choose and how much you consume.

Dietary fats, also known as fatty acids, come in two main types, saturated and unsaturated, but there is also a hybrid type—the now infamous *trans* fat. Think of saturated fats as the black-hat-wearing, gun-slinging bad guys in old matinee cowboy movies. They saunter into your body and cause all kinds of problems. Unsaturated fats are the white-hat heroes. They arrive to save the day and rescue your body from the ill effects of the saturated bad guys. And *trans* fats come straight from the science-fiction half of the matinee double bill. They're the mad scientists who create devastating weapons that can destroy everything, so they are best avoided.

Saturated fats. Saturated fats are bad because they cause the body to produce more artery-clogging cholesterol, which leads to coronary artery disease, heart attack, and stroke. Saturated fats are found mostly in animal products, are solid at room temperature, and have waxy textures. The white fat you see along the edge of or marbled throughout a piece of meat is saturated, as is the major type of fat found in the skin of poultry. Whole milk and milk products, such as butter, cheese, ice cream, and cream cheese, have saturated fats. You will also find saturated fats in certain tropical oils, such as palm oil, coconut oil, and cocoa butter.

Unsaturated fats. Unlike saturated fats, unsaturated fats are liquid at room temperature. There are two types of good-for-you unsaturated fats—monounsaturated and polyunsaturated. Monounsaturated fats are the best for you. They promote heart health and might help prevent cancer and other health problems. Monounsaturated fats lower low-density lipoprotein (LDL—the "bad" type) cholesterol levels without negatively affecting high-density lipoprotein (HDL—the "good" type) cholesterol levels. Canola oil, olive oil, and avocados are all good sources of monounsaturated fats, and the majority of fats found in most nuts are monounsaturated.

Polyunsaturated fats are moderately healthful. They can help lower your body's LDL cholesterol level, but they can also lower your body's HDL cholesterol level. Soybean oil, safflower oil, corn oil, cottonseed oil, and several other vegetable oils are high in polyunsaturated fat. Some nuts also contain fairly high levels of polyunsaturated fat.

Because unsaturated fats do not increase your total cholesterol level, they can help lower your risk of heart disease, heart attack, and stroke. Although nuts are terrific sources of unsatu-

How Much Fat Should You Eat?

The 2005 edition of *Dietary Guidelines for Americans* recommends getting between 20 percent and 35 percent of your calories from fat. That's between 40 and 70 grams of fat if you consume 2,000 calories a day. *Dietary Guidelines* also recommends getting less than 10 percent of your calories from saturated fat. The American Heart Association advises getting no more than 7 percent to 10 percent of your fat grams from saturated fat sources, and less than 1 percent (if any) from *trans* fat sources. The majority of your fat should come from unsaturated (monounsaturated and polyunsaturated) food sources.

rated fats, that doesn't mean you can eat as many as you want without consequence. High-fat foods should be eaten in moderation. See "How Much Fat Should You Eat?" on page 33 for information about your daily fat needs.

Trans fats. *Trans* fats are the worst type; most of them are manufactured by forcing hydrogen into liquid polyunsaturated fats in a process called hydrogenation (these fats are listed as partially hydrogenated oils in the ingredient list on food labels). The process produces solid fat products that have longer shelf lives and help stabilize the flavors in foods. Usual hangouts include shortening; some margarines (especially those in solid or stick form); fast-food favorites like French fries; and packaged cookies, cakes, chips, crackers, and similar snack foods.

Your body pays a big price when you consume large amounts of *trans* fats. They not only increase your body's production of cholesterol, but they also raise your LDL cholesterol level while lowering your HDL level. *Trans* fats have the most negative impact on your body.

When Fat & Cholesterol Collide

Cholesterol has become a dirty word because most people associate cholesterol with poor health. But without this fatty substance, your body couldn't function properly. The body uses cholesterol to produce healthy cells, make hormones, use vitamin D, and digest food. However, when your body has too much cholesterol, especially the wrong kind (LDL), you're at risk for atherosclerosis. This is a condition in which cholesterol and other substances form plaque deposits that constrict and harden the arteries, making it more difficult for blood to flow. But the real danger comes when plaque deposits break free and cause clots or block blood flow to parts of the body. That can leave those areas starving for oxygen and nutrients, possibly leading to a heart attack or a stroke.

You can get some cholesterol from your diet (dietary cholesterol), but your liver makes all the cholesterol you need. Dietary cholesterol is found only in protein-rich foods derived from animals, including eggs, red meat, poultry, fish, and dairy products. You will not find dietary cholesterol in

A Tale of Triglycerides

They don't get as much attention as cholesterol, but triglycerides are an important part of the fat equation. Your body uses some of the calories you eat for quick energy; the rest are stored as triglycerides in fat cells. If you eat more calories than you burn, you'll gain weight and likely have high triglyceride levels. Having high levels of triglycerides in your blood (more than 250 milligrams per deciliter of blood) can put you at risk for health problems like heart disease and stroke. But studies show nuts, when eaten on a regular basis, can lower triglyceride levels.

plant protein sources such as nuts, beans, soy products, and grains. Eating foods high in dietary cholesterol doesn't necessarily mean you'll have high blood-cholesterol levels. Saturated fat has more influence on blood-cholesterol levels; unfortunately, most foods of animal origin, especially meats and whole-milk products, are high in both saturated fat and dietary cholesterol.

Saturated fat is bad because it triggers the liver to make more cholesterol. Low-density lipoproteins (LDL, a certain combination of fat and protein) take cholesterol from the liver to the rest of the body. When you eat a lot of saturated fat, you increase the LDL cholesterol in your blood. The body doesn't dispose of most of this extra bad cholesterol. Instead, the LDL cholesterol gets left in the coronary arteries (the blood vessels that deliver oxygen and nutrients to the heart). This can lead to atherosclerosis and possibly a heart attack.

High-density lipoproteins (HDL, a different combination of fat and protein) work like a cholesterol vacuum because they pick up excess cholesterol in the blood and transport it back to the liver, which helps eliminate it from the body. That's why HDL cholesterol is the "good" type of cholesterol. You lower your risk of atherosclerosis and heart disease when your HDL cholesterol levels are higher and your LDL cholesterol levels are lower. For adults 20 and older, the National Cholesterol Education Program recommends you keep your total cholesterol level to less than 200 milligrams of cholesterol per deciliter of blood (mg/dL), your LDL cholesterol level less than 100 mg/dL, and your HDL cholesterol level more than 40 mg/dL to reduce the risk of heart disease. Speak with your doctor about your optimum cholesterol levels and any other heart-disease risk factors, such as smoking and family history of heart disease.

Nuts are a great cholesterol-free source of protein and are rich in unsaturated fat, which helps lower the amount of bad LDL cholesterol in the blood. So if you have high total and LDL cholesterol levels, nuts may help bring them down, particularly if you substitute nuts for snack foods high in saturated fat, such as chips, crackers, and cookies.

Get Cracking for Cardiovascular Health

Experts are convinced that nuts help your heart because they are high in unsaturated fat, but they also say nuts have other beneficial compounds, such as antioxidants. And research is backing up their claims. Here are a few of the most influential studies on nuts and the heart:

- One of the first major investigations into nuts and the heart was the Seventh-day Adventist Health Study. One of the founding principles of Seventh-day Adventists is that the body should be treated as God's temple. Members are encouraged to forego smoking, alcohol, and caffeine; to drink water; and to eat a predominantly plant-based diet. In a landmark 1992 study, researchers at Loma Linda University looked at 31,208 Seventh-day Adventists to study the relationship between their diets and heart health. They chose men and women who were at increased risk of developing heart disease or having a fatal heart attack (because of family history and other factors) and asked these people to list foods they frequently ate. Researchers discovered that participants who ate nuts four or more times a week had a lower chance of developing potentially fatal heart disease and had half the risk of having a heart attack, compared to participants who didn't eat nuts.

- The U.S. Physicians' Health Study has been following the health of its participants for nearly 20 years. One particular report from this study that was published in 2002 investigated how food choices influence heart health. A group of 21,454 participating men were given a questionnaire that asked how often they ate particular foods. Researchers followed up with the same men after one year and discovered that men who ate nuts two or more times a week, one ounce at a time, were 47 percent less likely to experience sudden cardiac death and were 30 percent less likely to die from coronary artery disease compared to the men who didn't consume nuts.

- A 2006 study in the *American Journal of Clinical Nutrition* investigated how a cholesterol-lowering diet compared to cholesterol-lowering drugs. The University of Toronto study followed 55 men and women who had high cholesterol levels. Twenty-nine of these adults had previously been on a one-month cholesterol-lowering program that included drugs called statins. Statins block the liver's ability to produce cholesterol and help the body reabsorb cholesterol so it can be eliminated. As a result, there is less cholesterol accumulating in the arteries. Common statins are atorvastatin (Lipitor), fluvastatin (Lescol), pravastatin (Pravachol), and simvastatin (Zocor). Study participants ate a plant-based diet that included almonds, margarine enhanced with plant sterols (more about sterols in the next section), soy protein, and fiber. After one year, cholesterol levels were reduced by 20 percent with the diet alone among those who complied. This was comparable to the effect attributed to cholesterol-lowering drugs.

The amount of evidence supporting the beneficial effects of nuts on heart health convinced the U.S. Food and Drug Administration (FDA) to approve a qualified health claim for certain nuts in 2003. Producers of almonds, walnuts, pecans, hazelnuts, pistachios, and peanuts can now say on their package labels and in ads that "scientific evidence suggests, but does not prove, that eating 1.5 ounces per day of most nuts, as part of a diet low in saturated fat and cholesterol, may reduce the risk of heart disease."

The Skinny on Sterols

Another reason nuts are good for you is that they contain small amounts of plant sterols. Sterols are waxy compounds found in the tissues of plants and animals. If the word sounds familiar, that's because cholesterol is a type of sterol. The plant sterols present in nuts are chemically related to the cholesterol found in animal protein.

Despite their chemical similarities, plant sterols and cholesterol have different effects on the body. Eating too much dietary cholesterol from animal sources can raise blood cholesterol levels, while plant sterols can lower them. Because they are similar in shape, plant sterols and animal cholesterol compete to be absorbed by the body. When the body absorbs plant sterols instead of cholesterol, the cholesterol is carried to the liver and eliminated. By blocking cholesterol, plant sterols help keep plaque from building up on artery walls, lessening the chance of heart disease, heart attack, and stroke.

Some food manufacturers are beginning to fortify certain foods like margarines with plant sterols for cholesterol-lowering effects, but experts are conservative about recommending these fortified foods. The American Heart Association advises that only people who currently have high blood-cholesterol levels or those who have already had a heart attack consume higher amounts of plant sterols. Health experts at the American Dietetic Association (ADA) encourage people to get the benefits of sterols by eating whole, natural foods known to contain them—like nuts.

A September 2006 study published in the *Journal of the American College of Cardiology* found that eating a handful of walnuts after a meal high in saturated fat blocked the body's absorption of cholesterol. The reasons for the protective effects aren't clear, but scientists suspect the unsaturated fats, antioxidants, and arginine (an amino acid that keeps plaque from forming on arteries) present in nuts play a big role.

Nuts & Diabetes

According to the American Diabetes Association, 20.8 million Americans have diabetes, a disease in which the body either doesn't produce enough or

properly use insulin.
Insulin is a hormone
that helps convert sugar
from the carbohydrates
in food into energy.
About 90 percent to
95 percent of people
with diabetes have type
2 diabetes, in which
cells don't produce
enough insulin or the
body ignores the insu-
lin cells do produce.
(Type 1 diabetes affects
5 percent to 10 percent
of people with diabetes.
With type 1 diabetes,
the body doesn't pro-

Check Those Peanut Butter Labels

Peanut butter is a great way to get all that good stuff in peanuts—but watch your labels. Most peanut butters are a mix of peanuts and vegetable oil. Look for the amount of saturated and unsaturated fat on the label. If there's more saturated fat per serving than unsaturated, you should choose a more healthful brand, or even make your own (see the next chapter).

duce insulin at all.) If you don't produce enough insulin or use it well, sugar builds in the blood and your cells are deprived of the fuel needed to produce energy. This sugar buildup can seriously damage the heart, eyes, kidneys, and nerves.

Diabetes is a fairly widespread condition, with about 7 percent of the American population affected, but more distressing are the estimated

54 million people who are considered predia-
betic—they have some insulin and sugar issues, but
they're not severe enough to warrant a diagnosis
of diabetes. However, studies are showing a direct
relationship between eating nuts or nut butters and
a lowered risk of diabetes.

The Harvard Nurses' Health Study has
followed the eating habits and health
of 86,016 women since 1980. When
researchers looked into the women's
nut consumption and their incidence of
diabetes, they found that those who ate
at least five ounces of nuts per week were 27 percent
less likely to develop type 2 diabetes than women
who rarely or never ate nuts. And women who ate a
tablespoon of peanut butter at least five times a week
were 21 percent less likely to develop diabetes.

Nuts & Cancer

The abundant antioxidants in nuts might lower
your risk of developing certain cancers. Antioxidants help protect cells from damage that can
lead to cancer. Nuts contain several antioxidants,
including vitamin E, ellagic acid, phytic acid, and
selenium (selenium is actually a mineral that contributes protective effects similar to antioxidants).

Several studies have suggested that antioxidants might lower cancer risk. One of the largest was the Chinese Cancer Prevention Study, which was published in 1993. This trial tested a combination of beta-carotene, vitamin E, and selenium on men and women who were at high risk for developing stomach cancer. According to the results, this antioxidant combination not only substantially lowered the risk of stomach cancer, but it also lowered the overall risk of developing cancer.

Other studies have found that eating nuts lowers the risk of developing prostate cancer. The amount of scientific evidence collected has been enough for the American Institute of Cancer Research to suggest people at risk for prostate cancer include nuts in their diet. Similar studies on colon cancer in women have also found that eating nuts on a regular basis has protective benefits.

There are many ongoing studies looking at the effects of certain antioxidants on cancer development. One of the largest is the Women's Health Study, which is set to conclude in 2009. This project is examining vitamin E and its potential protective effect against certain cancers, so even more amazing news about nuts and cancer might be on the horizon.

Other Nutty Benefits

Nuts seem to have even more health benefits than expected as researchers keep investigating how nuts affect a variety of problems. Smaller studies have shown that nuts might help with the following health issues.

Alzheimer's disease. Evidence is strong enough for the Alzheimer's Association to include nuts, specifically almonds, pecans, and walnuts, as part of its "Brain-Healthy Diet." The association points to nuts as a good source of the most active form of vitamin E, alpha-tocopherol. This cell-protecting antioxidant helps keep the building blocks of the brain healthy. Walnuts are also rich in melatonin, which research shows helps slow the progression of Alzheimer's disease.

Gallstones. A 2004 study published in the *American Journal of Clinical Nutrition* found that women who ate five or more ounces of nuts a week lowered their risk of developing gallstones. A similar study with men found that those who ate foods high in unsaturated fats were also less likely to develop gallstones.

Osteoporosis. Your bones may benefit from nuts, too. A 2007 study done at Penn State University concluded that specific nutrients such as alpha-linolenic acid (ALA), a type of the good-for-you omega-3 fatty acids in walnuts, may help keep bones from degrading over time and may actually make them stronger. The National Osteoporosis Foundation agrees that the omega-3 fatty acids found in walnuts help bones develop healthier and stay stronger.

Nutrition in a Nutshell

All nuts are healthful, but some are all-stars. Here are breakdowns of the essential nutrients in your favorite nuts and the reasons why they are so good for you. All nutritional values come from the U.S. Department of Agriculture (USDA National Nutrient Database for Standard Reference, Release 19). Daily Values (DV) are based on information from the FDA's Center for Food Safety and Applied Nutrition.

Winning Walnuts

Walnuts are one of the most-researched nuts, and all that study has concluded that they contain a unique combination of healthful fats and essential

English Walnut Nutritional Profile (per 1.5-ounce serving, or 21 walnut halves) 278 calories • total fat: 27.8 grams (43 percent of DV) • saturated fat: 2.6 grams (13 percent of DV) • monounsaturated fat: 3.8 grams • polyunsaturated fat: 20.1 grams • protein: 6.5 grams (13 percent of DV) • cholesterol: 0 milligrams • carbohydrate: 5.8 grams (2 percent of DV) • fiber: 2.8 grams (11 percent of DV) • calcium: 42 milligrams (4 percent of DV) • iron: 1.2 milligrams (7 percent of DV) • magnesium: 67 milligrams (17 percent of DV) • phosphorus: 147 milligrams (15 percent of DV) • potassium: 188 milligrams (5 percent of DV) • zinc: 1.31 milligrams (9 percent of DV) • copper: 0.7 milligram (35 percent of DV) • selenium: 2.1 micrograms (3 percent of DV) • manganese: 1.5 milligrams (75 percent of DV) • thiamin: 0.1 milligram (7 percent of DV) • riboflavin: 0.1 milligram (6 percent of DV) • niacin: 0.5 milligram (3 percent of DV) • vitamin B_6: 0.2 milligram (10 percent of DV) • vitamin E: 0.3 milligram (2 percent of DV) • vitamin C: 0.6 milligram (1 percent of DV)

nutrients. Many scientists say this combination contributes to some remarkable benefits.

Omega-3 fatty acids. Walnuts have more heart-healthful ALA omega-3 fatty acids than any other nut: They contain about 2.6 grams of ALA per ounce. ALA is a shorter omega-3 fatty acid than the type of omega-3 fat found in fatty fish (such as salmon and tuna), so it reacts a bit differently in the body.

In a study published in the January 16, 2007, edition of *Nutrition Journal,* researchers at Penn State University discovered that ALA found in walnuts might strengthen bones. A study in the September 2006 *Journal of the American College of Cardiology* found that the ALA-antioxidant combination in walnuts might protect the body from the artery-damaging effects of a meal loaded with satu-

What Are Daily Values?

Daily Values, which are referenced on all food labels, are a way of quantifying the amount of specific nutrients you need every day. They are based on the Recommended Dietary Allowances (RDA) for each nutrient and give you an idea of how a food contributes to your total recommended intake of nutrients. The U.S. Food and Drug Administration requested food manufacturers use Daily Values on food labels to make label reading less confusing. The percentages listed under "% DV" are based on a 2,000-calorie-a-day diet.

rated fat. In fact, studies have proven the type of omega-3 in walnuts lowers levels of LDL cholesterol and reduces the size of LDL cholesterol particles, making them less dangerous to your body. ALA has also been associated with keeping arteries healthier by reducing inflammation that can lead to plaque formation on artery walls.

Melatonin. A 2005 study done at the University of Texas Health Science Center showed that walnuts are a prime source of melatonin, an antioxidant that has been linked with a lower risk of cancer, less-severe heart disease, and improved brain function. Melatonin also has long been associated with better sleep.

Astonishing Almonds

Almonds are amazing nuts that may help you slim down. A roundup of studies on almonds and weight shows that the body may not absorb the fat in almonds (and other nuts might act similarly), so it doesn't contribute to weight gain. But that's not the only positive almond attribute.

Vitamin E. Almonds have more of the antioxidant vitamin E than any other nut. You can satisfy

Almond Nutritional Profile (per 1.5-ounce serving, or 36 almonds) 246 calories • total fat: 21.5 grams (33 percent of DV) • saturated fat: 1.7 grams (9 percent of DV) • monounsaturated fat: 13.7 grams • polyunsaturated fat: 5.2 grams • protein: 9 grams (18 percent of DV) • cholesterol: 0 milligrams • carbohydrate: 8.4 grams (3 percent of DV) • fiber: 5 grams (20 percent of DV) • calcium: 105 milligrams (11 percent of DV) • iron: 1.8 milligrams (10 percent of DV) • magnesium: 117 milligrams (29 percent of DV) • potassium: 310 milligrams (9 percent of DV) • phosphorus: 202 milligrams (20 percent of DV) • zinc: 1.4 milligrams (9 percent of DV) • copper: 0.5 milligram (25 percent of DV) • manganese: 1.1 milligrams (55 percent of DV) • selenium: 1.2 micrograms (2 percent of DV) • thiamin: 0.1 milligram (7 percent of DV) • riboflavin: 0.3 milligram (18 percent of DV) • niacin: 1.7 milligrams (9 percent of DV) • vitamin B_6: 0.1 milligram (3 percent of DV) • vitamin E: 11 milligrams (55 percent of DV)

55 percent of your daily vitamin E needs in a one-and-a-half-ounce serving of almonds. And almonds contain alpha-tocopherol, the important type of vitamin E that the National Academy of Science deems the most active in the human body. Studies have linked alpha-tocopherol with lowered cholesterol levels, reduced risk of some cancers,

fewer complications from diabetes, a stronger immune system, and a healthier brain.

Magnesium. Almonds are also a rich source of magnesium, a mineral that keeps your bones healthy, helps your nerves and muscles function properly, keeps your blood pressure down, and prevents heart rhythm abnormalities. A 2006 study conducted by researchers at North-western University that was published in the journal *Circulation* suggested that getting enough magnesium in your diet can reduce your risk factors for developing heart disease and diabetes.

Potent Peanuts

Science is giving the nod to the health properties of the beloved goober. According to a 2004 study published in the *American Journal of Clinical Nutrition,* women whose diet provided them with half of their fat (which was mostly unsaturated) coming from peanuts, peanut butter, and peanut oil reduced their risk of heart disease by 14 percent compared with women who ate a lower-fat diet that didn't include peanuts. The women who ate the diet that was rich in

Peanut Nutritional Profile (per 1.5-ounce serving, or 42 peanuts) 241 calories • total fat: 20.9 grams (32 percent of DV) • saturated fat: 2.9 grams (15 percent of DV) • monounsaturated fat: 10.4 grams • polyunsaturated fat: 6.6 grams • protein: 11 grams (22 percent of DV) • cholesterol: 0 milligrams • carbohydrate: 7 grams (2 percent of DV) • fiber: 3.6 grams (14 percent of DV) • calcium: 39 milligrams (4 percent of DV) • iron: 2 milligrams (11 percent of DV) • magnesium: 71 milligrams (18 percent of DV) • potassium: 300 milligrams (9 percent of DV) • phosphorus: 160 milligrams (16 percent of DV) • zinc: 1.4 milligrams (9 percent of DV) • copper: 0.5 milligram (25 percent of DV) • selenium: 3.1 micrograms (4 percent of DV) • manganese: 0.8 milligram (40 percent of DV) • thiamin: 0.3 milligram (20 percent of DV) • riboflavin: 0.1 milligram (6 percent of DV) • niacin: 5.1 milligrams (26 percent of DV) • vitamin B_6: 0.1 milligram (5 percent of DV) • folate: 102 micrograms (26 percent of DV) • vitamin E: 3.5 milligrams (17 percent of DV)

peanuts and unsaturated fat lost the same amount of weight as the women who ate the lower-fat diet.

Fiber. Peanuts are legumes, and all legumes are good sources of fiber. Fiber is a carbohydrate that you can't digest, so it goes in and out of your body without being stored for use. But when fiber goes, it helps move waste through your intestines, keeping you regular, and keeping harmful germs from setting up shop. The type of fiber found in legumes can also help remove cholesterol from your body and reduce your risk for heart disease.

Powerful Pecans

Research is linking the consumption of pecans with lower cholesterol levels, and this nut is a potent antioxidant source. Pecans are rich in zinc, copper, magnesium, and manganese, minerals that help support the body's antioxidant defense system.

Manganese. One serving of pecans provides almost your entire daily requirement of this essential mineral. Manganese aids in keeping your brain, blood, and bones healthy; helps your body better use calcium; and helps regulate blood-sugar levels. Manganese is considered an antioxidant, so it may help keep your arteries healthy and lower your risk of cancer.

With all the benefits nuts provide, you'll be eager to find ways to work them into your diet more often.

Pecan Nutritional Profile (per 1.5-ounce serving, or 30 pecan halves) 294 calories • total fat: 30.6 grams (47 percent of DV) • saturated fat: 2.6 grams (13 percent of DV) • monounsaturated fat: 17.4 grams • polyunsaturated fat: 9.2 grams • protein: 3.9 grams (8 percent of DV) • cholesterol: 0 milligrams • carbohydrate: 5.9 grams (2 percent of DV) • fiber: 4.1 grams (16 percent of DV) • calcium: 30 milligrams (3 percent of DV) • iron: 1.1 milligrams (6 percent of DV) • magnesium: 51 milligrams (13 percent of DV) • potassium: 174 milligrams (5 percent of DV) • phosphorus: 118 milligrams (12 percent of DV) • zinc: 1.9 milligrams (13 percent of DV) • copper: 0.5 milligram (25 percent of DV) • selenium: 1.6 micrograms (2 percent of DV) • manganese: 1.9 milligrams (95 percent of DV) • thiamin: 0.3 milligram (20 percent of DV) • riboflavin: 0.1 milligram (6 percent of DV) • niacin: 0.5 milligram (3 percent of DV) • vitamin B_6: 0.1 milligram (5 percent of DV) • folate: 9 micrograms (2 percent of DV) • vitamin E: 0.6 milligram (3 percent of DV)

You'll find tips in the next chapter for selecting and storing nuts, and you'll learn how they can complement your favorite foods.

Easy Ways to Become a Health Nut

Okay, you're convinced—nuts are good for you. They keep your heart healthy; help protect against chronic disease; and provide protein, fiber, and essential vitamins and minerals. Working these nutritious gems into your diet is easy. All it takes is a little know-how, some common sense, and a bit of creativity.

Buying the Best

Your first buying choice is relatively simple—unshelled or shelled. Whichever way you go, you need to take a close look at what you're purchasing.

Unshelled nuts should have intact shells—no cracks, holes, or blemishes. They should feel heavy and should be fairly uniform in size. Make sure that in-shell nuts are fresh and ripe before you buy them by picking up and shaking a few. If the nuts rattle in the shell, they're likely old or underdeveloped.

If shelled nuts please the eye, they should please the palate. Look for plump, similarly sized, uniformly colored nuts.

Once you've mastered the shell game, you still have loads of choices. Knowing the basics makes choosing the right nut a bit easier.

Raw. This is your pure nut, as close to its natural form as you can get. It's best to buy raw nuts when they're as fresh as possible. If you live in a nut-growing region, buy nuts in-season from local sources. If you don't have nut farms in your area, ask your market manager how often bulk nuts are shipped and sold. If you buy raw nuts that are in bags, check labels for sell-by dates.

Roasted. Roasted nuts are raw, usually shelled, and have been baked in an oven (about 350 degrees Fahrenheit) for 10 to 20 minutes. Roasted nuts are typically seasoned with salt, but you can find unsalted varieties, which are better for keeping your blood pressure down. Roasting brings out the flavor of the nut, which makes them great sprinkled on your favorite salad.

You can buy dry-roasted or oil-roasted nuts. You'd think oil-roasted nuts would be much fattier than dry-roasted ones, but there's really little difference in fat content. Oil-roasted nuts might have one extra gram of fat. The differences are more personal: Dry-roasted nuts are typically crispier, while oil-roasted nuts have a slicker mouth feel.

Roast Your Own

A great, healthy way to enjoy nuts is to buy the raw materials, roast them yourself, and add your own special twist. Roasting nuts brings out their flavor without adding unneeded fat. Take this basic roasted nut recipe and add your favorite spices.

Preheat your oven to 350 degrees. Spread ⅔ of a cup of your favorite raw nuts on a baking sheet and sprinkle with a pinch of salt and/or other spices (if desired). Roast for ten minutes. Let cool.

Toasted. Toasted nuts are similar to roasted ones, but toasted raw shelled nuts are heated at a higher temperature (about 400 degrees Fahrenheit) for a shorter amount of time (five to ten minutes). You can toast nuts on your stovetop, too. Heat your skillet over medium heat, add shelled raw nuts, and toast for five to ten minutes. You can add a little oil if you need to. Like roasting, this technique brings out a more intense flavor.

Blanched. Blanched nuts are raw shelled nuts boiled in water for two to three minutes and then immediately taken out and rinsed with cold water. This cooking process also intensifies the flavor (although blanching typically produces a milder taste than roasting or toasting) and gives nuts vibrant colors. Blanched nuts are great when added to stir-fried dishes or sprinkled on top of baked goods, such as muffins.

Salted or unsalted. Salt brings out the flavor of nuts, but watch your amounts. Eating too much salt has been linked to high blood pressure and may cause the body to get rid of calcium. The latest version of *Dietary Guidelines for Americans* recommends getting no more than 2,400 milligrams of sodium a day—that's about a teaspoon of salt. A one-and-a-half-ounce serving of salted, dry-roasted peanuts has about 346 milligrams of salt (compared to 3 milligrams in the unsalted variety). If you're on a restricted-sodium diet, or if you are salt-sensitive, you should buy unsalted nuts.

Candied. If you're a fan of sweet treats, candied nuts are for you—in moderation, of course. These shelled nuts (which are usually raw, but you can candy roasted, toasted, or blanched nuts, too) are dunked in a syrup. The syrup is made by melting sugar (and usually a flavoring, such as vanilla) in a saucepan over medium heat. Just as the sugar melts, the raw nuts are stirred in and quickly removed, then placed on a baking sheet to dry.

Proper Storage—In Shell or Out

Most nuts can last years if you store them properly. Unshelled nuts should be stored in an airtight  container, such as a resealable freezer-safe bag or other plastic container (avoid metal containers; metal can cause nuts to go rancid). Most unshelled nuts will last eight months when stored in the refrigerator, but they will keep for as long as three years in the freezer. Shelled nuts are a bit more fragile. Stored in an airtight container, shelled nuts will last about four months in the fridge. If frozen, shelled nuts can last as long as two years.

Improperly stored nuts can become rancid because they contain so much fat. If exposed to air or heat for too long, the fat chemically changes. This chemical change causes nuts to smell and taste putrid or "off." They'll also soften and change colors. Nuts' biggest enemies are light, humidity, heat, and metal. That's why it's a smart move to store your nuts in plastic in the fridge or the freezer, and not at room temperature.

Adding Nuts to Your Diet

Although the scientific community promotes the healthful power of nuts, experts are clear—you should indulge in moderation. The latest version of *Dietary Guidelines for Americans* recommends getting 20 percent to 35 percent of your calories from fat—and goes further to state that most of those fat grams should come from unsaturated fat sources, such as nuts. But even good fat is full of calories, and excess calories can pack on unnecessary pounds. A single one-and-a-half-ounce serving (about one-third cup) of nuts can satisfy as much as a third of your fat needs for the entire day. So go nuts in moderation, and try the following ideas to add nuts to your menu.

Breakfast

The powerful nutrition punch of nuts will get any day started off right. Best of

> **Did You Know...**
>
> You shouldn't store your nuts near onions, fish, or garlic. Nuts tend to absorb the odors of strongly flavored foods.

all, they're a simple, quick addition to the breakfast foods you are already eating each morning.

- Add a sprinkle of your favorite nuts on top of your yogurt or your favorite cereal.

- Try adding nuts to your favorite muffin or coffee cake recipe.

- Sprinkle nuts over your oatmeal for a heart-healthful double whammy.

- Make a parfait by layering low-fat yogurt, fresh fruit, and nuts.

Lunch

Nuts are great for a midday pick-me-up. The extra protein will fuel you throughout the afternoon so you can keep cracking.

- Make nuts a regular addition to your lunchtime salad. It doesn't have to be a green salad because nuts are also a flavorful addition to pasta and chicken salads.

- Sprinkle nuts over your favorite creamy soup.

- Instead of eating your usual side of chips, try a handful of mixed nuts or a trail mix of nuts and dried fruit.

- Blend chopped nuts into low-fat cream cheese, and use it as a spread on bread or crackers.

Dinner

If you strayed from your healthful diet during the day and indulged in a little too much saturated fat, finish the day on a high note with nuts.

- Add nuts to a stir-fry dish, and cook it in your favorite nut oil.

- Top your side dishes with nuts. Pasta dishes, rice dishes, and even vegetables will get some crunch and an added flavor boost.

- Grind nuts in a blender or food processor, and blend them with breadcrumbs for a nutty breading for chicken or fish.

- Sprinkle chopped nuts over a fresh-fruit medley for a light dessert.

Make Your Own Nut Butter

Most commercial brands of nut butter add oil and sugar—oil to make the butter spread more easily, and sugar to make it more pleasing to young palates. If you'd like a healthier spread, make your own nut butter. And you don't have to stick with peanuts; just substitute your favorite nut in this recipe from the National Peanut Board.

Combine two cups of roasted, shelled, unsalted peanuts with one tablespoon of oil (preferably peanut oil) and a half-teaspoon of salt (if desired). Put all ingredients in a food processor or blender, and blend for two to three minutes (scraping sides occasionally). Put in an airtight container, and store in your refrigerator. The oil may separate when refrigerated, so you should stir well before spreading. Also, homemade nut butter does not spread as well as the commercial variety, so take it out of the fridge and let it sit for a few minutes at room temperature to make spreading easier.

Whether you're a nut novice or a nut connoisseur, you can feel good about adding nuts to your diet. Every time you grab a handful of nuts as a snack or to add sparkle to a favorite recipe, remember you are doing something good for your health.